CW01656589

The Wonder of Merlin

Ancient Wisdom and Teachings for Enlightenment

RoseAnne Rosslin

THE WONDER OF MERLIN
Ancient Wisdom and Teachings for Enlightenment
Copyright © 2023 RoseAnne Rosslin

The moral rights of the author have been asserted.
All rights reserved. No part of this book may be used or reproduced or transmitted in any manner without prior written permission, except in the case of 'fair use' brief quotations embodied in articles and reviews.

The unauthorised reproduction or distribution of this copyright work is illegal. No part of this book may be scanned, uploaded, or distributed via the Internet or any other means, graphic, electronic, or mechanical, including photocopying, print, recording, taping, or by any storage retrieval system without the author's permission.

Cover Design by RoseAnne Rosslin © 2023

Published by RoseAnne Rosslin
www.roseannerosslin.com
info@roseannerosslin.com

E-Book ISBN: 978-1-9164735-7-7
Paperback ISBN: 978-1-9164735-6-0

CONTENTS

Introduction by RoseAnne

With my recent move to living in a remote rural location with very little interruption, the energy and power of Merlin enveloped me and persisted to such an extent that it could not be ignored or put aside. Merlin requested I channel his words to encourage 'the people' to use their magic within, their spirit to connect with their higher beings, the 'all of you'.

I first knowingly received the energy of Merlin some thirty years ago, when a vision appeared to me from the magician we know as Merlin along with magical, mystical, and otherworldly visions and communication that unfolded through my practice as a medium and in my meditations. Although it was only recently that I started to write his words, his story unfolded, and I learned more about his lifetime on Earth.

Merlin made his true presence fully known to me with a distinct and memorable visit. He appeared to me as he had been for the latter part of his lifetime on Earth, an elderly man with long matted wild hair, and a tall wooden crook in tattered robes scattered with leaves. Since then, he now appears to me as the mighty magician from the Spirit world, full of wisdom, calming and a bright light, seeking my recognition to work with him and write his words.

Merlin has also previously visited me in a variety of ways to show me there are many aspects to the one man that lived on Earth who has historically been known as Merlin, and many channellers see him differently with a variety of talents, including the wizard's magic powers with potions and spells. The Merlin that visits me from the Spirit world is not about spells, but the magnificence of the Earth world, the forgotten magic within Mother Earth and the heavenly surroundings on Earth.

Throughout the years, I have encountered many fairy-like creatures around me and also witnessed their colours in nature, mostly in the forests and by the sea. Since Merlin has become a stronger presence in my life for channelling his words, I am regularly visited by elemental beings that appear in many ways, but I know with all my heart they exist in a most beautiful and special way, that I feel very privileged to see and in a small way be connected with their world to share with others.

The channellings have come through to assist with the growth of human consciousness and help bring about a more profound awareness of other unseen life forms on Earth. Thus, creating a shift to living a purer life with nature, learning how to live with oneself, to know your way and be conscious and respectful of the other realms that exist side by side with the human race.

Within the book, Merlin gives insights and descriptions of his life and experience of living with Spirit on Earth. He passes on potent wisdom, guidance, and teachings on how to live a spiritual life in the physical world and relays channellings that may seem like far-fetched stories, so I suggest the words are read with an open mind to all the possibilities of this world as when the words were delivered, I felt no surprise, only the truth of what is and that there is far more life on Earth than we can comprehend.

It is worth noting that as with my first two books, the message of caring for Mother Earth also runs strongly throughout these channellings from Merlin. It has become very apparent that this is a message Spirit has requested I deliver, as it is highly significant to Spirit, Elementals and Entities that we take care of our planet Earth, along with our spiritual being.

With love and light, RoseAnne.

Introduction by Merlin

In this book of my learnings from Earth and beyond, I refer to 'you' the reader, unless stated 'the writer'. I want to talk to those that will read my words and pass on the knowledge I learnt in my existence, known to the many as Merlin the magician.

As you will note from my words, I was a soul that had lost my way and, through this experience, I found my way and being on Earth. The existence was a great one for me as I learnt to live with the magic of the Earth and Spirit folded in one. It was not easy at first and as I discovered myself, I became clear and could unfold my magic within.

Spells are not my way, potions are not my way, although I can work with the plants and herbs, and more, my way is Spirit. I worked with my spirit and the spirit of the Earth, this is the magic you all seek and however it is wrapped up for you, Spirit exists more than you can see. It is an energy that guides you all. Realise you are a body of Earth, matter enfolded with Spirit. It is the spirit of you that is the magic.

Therefore, my overall message to your readers is to follow a purposeful and more enlightened path. This is so that the Earth world can progress in light and the harmony of each kingdom within the Earth world can connect, which will also help the growth of the spiritual world within Earth and without.

It is time for the people to develop their own 'technology' as given by God, the creator, the divine, the One being that must now govern your way and this book is intended for this purpose, to inspire, enlighten, and provide knowledge and wisdom that is being widely forgotten in the development of the technological world. The electronic light is held in high regard, but it is the light within the human that is the everlasting and sustenance you seek.

As you are all at different stages on your spiritual path, we, the Spirit world, know some of you may understand these words, and others may dismiss these words and some may ignore the words and some may misunderstand these words. So, in this book, there are brief explanations with conclusions for each channelling, emphasising the main message along with guidance for living your life with Spirit.

We understand the variety of the human form, and the difference in your characters, personalities, the uniqueness of each of you and the speciality you bring to the Earth world that makes the world an abundance of variety that stands out in the galaxy. We know you each hold opinions, meanings, and interpretations of these words and will take up the words at different times and in different locations, but with each reading, whether you acknowledge or comprehend, you expand your consciousness. As with each letter typed that makes up the words, the sentences into stories and teachings, they are lessons for your being, a reminder that you are more than the physical, more than the reflection in your mirrors and more than you can possibly conceive from a dimension of spiritual limitation.

So, do not fathom out or question too much the words you read, just be in the vibration of the words that have come through spirit to your spirit. Like telephoning your best friend, we come in love to pass on wisdom, inspiration, and most of all, love. Let the love soak into your being, knowing we are here for all who read the words. We surround you to enfold you in our love and your being will be refreshed, your mind united with One and your heart renewed in the light of these words. Even if the words do not resonate with your physical mind at this time, they whisper words you know from a previous 'time' from a higher place of being that you will remember in time.

With love and blessings, Merlin.

CHAPTER ONE

My Life on Earth as Merlin

The Way

The mystical, magical figures history has portrayed is quite different from who I really was, a hermit living in caves and hills hiding out from the human life existence and retreating to the nature of Earth, where I felt more at ease, comfortable with who I was, the magician of Earth.

This does not mean wands or even potions, although I used herbs, seeds, and flowers of the earth to heal. I mean the ability to foresee the future, to know intuitively where to live to bear fruit, to heal people's hearts and nature, and to look into souls and see their dreams and wishes, and know the way they should travel, the best direction to complete their life's purpose and journey.

I was a wizard of the mind and heart and knew how to work with rock, animals, soil, and plants, of all nature. I was born into a life of knowing. The stars, Sun and Moon are part of the Earth, but it was the Earth itself that I knew and therefore lived with the Earth in amongst the trees, soil, rock, and plants, which brought mother nature to my door of other worlds, the mystical nature of the other beasts, the fairy world, and the dragon world.

My life in the wild connected me with my dragon elemental, a powerful and commanding dragon that has a lot of wisdom and potent guidance, and who accompanied me throughout my life on Earth. All of which you have encountered (the writer) and now we take a hold, a grip and focus on the world of magic, the other beings that share your Earth, the winged creatures of the night and day, we start the journey to seeing the mysterious creatures who create wonders amongst you, the human.

Do not be discouraged if these words disappoint you with my portrayal of your spoon-fed history of who you thought I was, the magic portrayed by many stories is all that is required to uplift you and inspire you. Therefore, I am honoured to have been presented to the world as a magician of importance. But remember, the magic lies within you for the magic to be displayed before your eyes.

Within this book, I will skip around the elemental worlds as there are varying levels of elemental life forms and rather than give you a dictionary and explanation of each, which I do not want to do, it is better to have a general understanding and introduction to Mother Nature's little workers that will help you help Spirit with taking care of the planet.

Who Am I?

The Merlin, is the name on the modern man's lips and you all know instantly who I am, the wizard, the magician, the magical guardian of King Arthur. Not so, I was the magician of the creator, the divine energies. I worked with no man till I had conquered my energy in the wild, amongst the hills and if I encountered men, then I assisted in their journeys and if they were kings, princes, or working men or women then my light and ways were needed by the people.

History has made a mockery of my life, but the essence is in truth. I lived like a nomad, wondered the hills looking for truth and found it; that is magic. My name is Merlin today and Merdith yesterday and I wondered from coast line to coast line and left a trail of my existence as my story through time has left a power of strength and courage. I strayed from the Britain you know to a country over the sea, Ireland and over to the French coast, and back to England up into the high lands of Scotland, and on each encounter of my travels I met men in need of my truth, which I passed on and became folklore and legend and stories of healing and magic.

My staff was made of wood and my stones were like runes, a tool to expand my consciousness to see beyond the physical picture. I reflected each day in an energy I had found, not of a mortal nature, not of this world, and I could leave my body and astral project, although I believed this to be living and dying. So, when I would awake from where I had been, I was refreshed in a new energy, the God energy, but to me it was the nature of truth, the true nature. I had become blessed in my search for truth and the elementals helped bless my nature. They encouraged me to wander the land to seek new ways and energies and to walk amongst them to learn more of their ways to help man with his health, to learn how to nurture the earth and to take care of their own beasts within the human self, so the elementals could live in peace with the human.

Man's ways changed, the greed of land and riches, the rivalry between siblings in power, the fight to survive with the most became power, not the power of your natural selves, and so my ways were ignored by the men of influence and I was made a fairy tale, a song of peace and love. Yet, truth is strong, so now your nature (man) has turned into gold and greed. However, this is changing drastically, as the Earth turns and the disasters increase, man is looking to his higher self, his truest nature to exist with the Earth and not against its physical ruler, the Earth. Life has become more about witches, wizards, and higher beings than the magic within oneself. You are all born with magic.

Again, we say uplift your spirits with the knowledge; I was more a magician of the Earth with the great power to see other worldly realms existing within the Earth realm, something that is important to remember as you walk through the villages, the towns, the cities, and the industrial estates man has made wielding great power and fumes that choke and exhaust you all.

Seek clean air and you will breathe life back into this world. Seek clean spiritual air and you will breathe life back into you.

My Name

A name has power in your world, but in mine, I am spirit, and have lived many times with many names. I do have a name for my greater spirit, but let us stay with the picture you live in, so the focus is clear. It is the magic of Earth that this book is about, and using your magic inside of you with the Earth. Take note the name Merlin is the modern man's name for me. This is the name used to recognise my work on Earth, then so be it.

The name you have been given by birth can change or alter throughout your life for different stages of your growth or development. Your birth name is a root to who you are, remember there are many roots to who you are.

My name as Merlin is a power man has created to bring in my energy to empower their assistance with spirituality, magic, and wonder. This is a powerful tool and a powerful source as I am not one, I am more than one, but I am with the One, so thinking or speaking of my name creates a magical presence of a beautiful harmony into your world. Let it be so.

Let the words of this book bring in and enfold you with ancient knowledge, wisdom, and enlightenment. All the ingredients of mystery, but this is not so; there is no mystery. It is all at your fingertips surrounding you today.

The Day I First Saw the Elementals

Like you (the writer) I saw colours and wisps of energy flying by, and in my inner eye I could see as clear as day the characters in various forms of fairies, insect-like creatures, and little men-like beings. Until, one day, they became real to my outer eye and in all their glory, revealed their shape and form to sit with me and communicate their ways. They told me why they were showing their true beings and how I had adjusted to their energies and could be trusted to work with them.

They are ancient beings having developed with the Earth and part of the creator's energy to assist the earth and animals and the evolution of the Earth. They are magical in part and a counterpart of the human in part, and very much a part of the insect world with wings and tails and eyes that see a different world. They live in trees, huddled in roots, bushes, and caves, high in the mountains and rocks of the sea, an underworld of the sea. They sparkle and glow, move quickly and spring from one place to another, whereas some walk and move in lightning strokes from one place to another. They are fascinating, worldly, and pure in nature.

But not all, some have become malformed with nature's ways and man's interruption of the skyline and depths of the sea. The earth being polluted has moved them away from their homes, out of their lands and damaged by man's waste. In my time, it was the bloodshed and war, the hatred man poured out into the land, the fighting, the killing that destroyed some of their sparkle to create the mischievous, misbehaved beings of man's counterpart, a part of themselves on the fairy creatures.

With the surge of spiritual consciousness, awareness and the light being spread amongst you as a race, it has restored some of their light too and their willingness to work more with mankind to help you to help them heal Mother Earth.

To see a fairy is a God given gift. To communicate with a fairy is beyond the human ken. To believe in fairies is still a tale of magic. There are many variants of the fairy and many fairies that live amongst you in land that is rich and clean. Respect the elemental part of you as your body is sprung from their nature.

My Life Amongst the Hills

As you (the writer) are now in amongst the hills and mountains, but comfortably so, this is where I lived and remained at my best, undisturbed by human life and happy to live in nature with the nature elements. To look out on vistas that stretched as far as the eye could see with no man; this was the peace and solitude I needed to do my work.

I studied the life of the animals in the forest, from the wild boar to the ants; they were my friends. The birds flew in flocks far larger than you have now and the trees grew taller and wider with richer soil and filled with vibrancy. It was a land filled with magical surprises, plants and growth that had not been stolen by man and grew in abundance on the land. But ignorance prevented the people from resourcing the forest, not all, but many did not know what lay beneath the soil or high in the trees for their goodness. I had a natural instinct for such things, and I replenished my body with fruits, seeds and plants grown naturally from the ground, pure and free. My habitat was rock, and the caves provided shelter and warmth from the harsh weather and the burning heat; we had both, but more in alignment with the natural seasons.

As I gained in strength through knowledge of the land, what to eat and where to go, who to trust and what to believe, I became a nature spirit myself. I connected a part of me with nature so deep within, I could communicate and live amongst nature spirits who recognised me as one of them in human form. To do this was a remarkable and fascinating feat for me. I loved, honoured, and respected the little folk of the night and day, that live amongst you all, unseen by the majority and only viewed by the minority. My tongue could speak with them and I was respected by them to know and see their magical powers at work. It was magic to me as turning a leaf in colour, changing the curve of a branch, flying amongst the leaves and flowers, creating harmony to each to care and nurture a plant is magical and mysterious.

How did their nature appear? Where do they come from? What is their life span and how do they recreate?

They are the best of humans. They are focused on life, Earth life and animal life. Their nature and beings know only one thing: their energy is pure, unsullied by intellect, only a form of spirit, a creature of Mother Earth.

Mother nature is your healer and lover for the human spirit, mind, and body. Find time with nature, observe the animals, be with animals and be at one with your earthly friends that you do not see, knowing they go about their work taking care of planet Earth for all living upon Earth.

The elementals love to play with the children; they love to play with the young animals and they love the adults who can find their inner child and be joyful and kind in their nature. They feel the human's energy more than some of you can know yourself, and they know the energy of a human's respect for their own being and the Earth.

CHAPTER TWO

The Elemental World of Earth

More About the Fairy Folk

I call them nature spirits, but so you understand the difference between the different elementals, I am talking here about the forest fairies as there are many nature spirits, some I never knew as I did not live at sea or high in the mountains or on dry moorland or amongst the air, but I know the water spirits, the forest spirits and the nature spirits that take care of the plants and animals.

They dance at night amongst the trees and rest mostly in the day. They live a certain length of time of varying degrees, but for a very long time, sometimes a century or more, to see out their purpose, then they dissipate into the ether to be a part of the where the creator creates. They are born out of the Earth and replicated by each group of beings. They grow into their nature like plants, flowers and trees or surround groups of animals and live amongst the insects. They generate harmony and a balance in the land by their very being. Like a farmer taking care of its animals or clearing the land or debris, so do these spirits of nature. They are playful and full of light and there are those that are naughty, mischievous and have strayed from their essence and become non-playful and tricksters, these are the ones that can play havoc with the unbalanced human or where there is neglect or dark in the human being. They are unable to create any more power than play on your feelings, misbehaving has become their nature, but this reflects the human world that creates mischief and disrespect to oneself.

The spiritual light on Earth is important for the nature spirits too, with their development and upkeep of the planet. To extinguish parts of nature is very sad for the animals that have to find new homes or a new way of life. This is reflected amongst the nature spirits too, even as man mows his lawn and treats his weeds with pesticide they hide, they disappear.

If you believe, if you know in your heart that amongst you are beautiful energies of spirits nature taking care of the

Earth, preserve your grass in a corner for them to live, let the grass grow, nurture the wild land with them, with your hands, let the insects live there and the grass grow. Be a part of a higher nature.

The Magic in the Air

Invisible vibrations and moving waves of electronic substance and radiation disturb the Earth's natural atmosphere. Although there are many benefits to the new man's way of life, the disruption to the ecological balance, the environment as I experienced it, has changed the way the elementals work with the air, and the particles of the atmosphere have changed. What was pure has become impure with the dramatic increase of pollution, so how does this affect the nature spirits of the air?

Where do they go to avoid the polluted air?

They don't; they have a pure air that they exist in, but it is now in limited amounts. The ether changes as your planet changes.

Impossible, you say, why?

The nature spirits are just that, part of nature and close to nature and just next door to your planet, they exist on your planet, surrounding your planet and some are choking as the smog, chemicals, and other substances that you know nothing of pollute the air. So, this is changing their existence and habitat. Places on Earth that are untouched by the large buildings and chemical atmosphere, the factories, and industrial buildings, have life in abundance of the nature spirits; where there is green, there is life from the elementals. They cannot exist in bricks and mortar with unnatural heat and man-made smells that pollute the air. They can exist in your homes where there is less heat, where there is less pollution, and they can bring joy and life to your homes. Inspiration is their gift to you. Happiness and brightness of spirit is their nature. Joy is their natural state of being. They know nothing of your worries as the creator provides, the creator gives, the creator is and they know it, and exist in this energy, purposefully creating more of 'His' energy. It is another world amongst the nature spirits and respect from humans is needed to bring about the visions and helpful nature of these beautiful beings.

How do you work with the elementals to help you to help them?

Be bold and believe they are all around you, everything you touch and feel they know. Fill your home with green, let nature into your house, bring in the plants from outside to inside and oxygenate, purify the air with the plants. The plants attract the sprightly beings to live and provide you with cleaner air, and just as you watch the bee collecting pollen from a plant, the sprites are energised by plant life and it is vital for their homes. Nurture these plants knowing they are helping you and, in turn, helping the nature spirits help you. They exist to be part of you, not to be ignored and shunned from the homes. They have lost a lot of the Earth in the increase of man's new way of life. It has changed their existence. There will always be the nature spirits where nature exists at its best. Between the Spirit world and the Earth world, there is another world of existence of untold beauty and good-hearted creatures living in a world of truth, the communicators of Spirit.

Pollution not only affects man, animals, and the life on Earth, it affects the nature of the elementals; it destroys the equilibrium between worlds on Earth. To bring back a cleaner environment and put balance back into the world you know as planet Earth, a change in awareness and activity is required.

Expand your consciousness and knowledge to help all living on the planet. Let Spirit help and guide each of you to do what you can, where you are, and build a new way of living, brighter, cleaner, and sustainable. Breathe life into the planet.

The Snow

The joy of snow and the curse of snow. The joy of snow is the feeling of purity, the magic and beauty of the peaceful snow until it turns frosty, icy, and bitter, blizzards and cumbersome, sloshy, and slippery. But when it falls from the sky like magic stars separating on the ground and lying softly, crunching gently beneath your feet, it feels a delight and the lovable, childlike nature emerges from the depths of you. But not for all and not all like the scenes of snow, fearing the worst it can bring.

With the winter season, there is a higher purpose to the snowfall. Its flakes are distinct and unique like all of you individually, myriads of you sprinkled over the Earth like individual flakes of snow.

So, what is the higher purpose? What is the magic of snow? What is the wonder of snow?

It is water and therefore the nymphs and water sprites are working hard across the land, keeping the balance of nature at one with the Earth turning in its sunlight. The miracle of each season is controlled by the weather patterns, created by the Earth, and influenced by man.

The Universe has its part to play too, but this seems ignored on the whole; scientists not realising the air on Pluto, if disturbed, raises the pollution on Earth.

What nonsense is this you may think? Can Uranus affect the weather on Earth, Venus or Mars have a gravitational pull on the Earth that it twirls a different way? Who can measure with the accuracy required to provide the proof?

It's here and it's coming. The scientists that watch the planets with Earth know and leak out only what you need to know. There is a lot more hidden information of scientific facts that would seem impossible for you to absorb and alter the change in global pollution and warming. Devastations blamed for planetary misalignment and goings on in the night sky that you have no idea of that affect the planet Earth.

So, how does this affect the snow?

In quantities and quality, there is a difference in the quality of snow across the planet. There are caves of snow on Earth with snow giants that dictate how much snow will appear as they work extremely hard at balancing the snow with the planet's air quality and correlate with rain and wind and sun. They integrate and measure to keep Earth coated in a cloth of snow for animals, for extremes of heat and for survival of the sea and the fish kingdom. The snow giants are air and earth and water collecting, removing, and measuring the precious snow that is now becoming a commodity in certain places. They are not harmful; they exist like the wind giants who are harmful to man and living creatures suffer at the harm of the wind giants who anger with the destruction of the planet by man. The snow giants are gentle beasts although their intent is to bring a protection to the land, but many suffer under the hands of the snow.

Each elemental on a large scale for air, fire, water, and the earth have many off-springs who do good for the land and sea. Overall, man cannot see them, and only tales exist, and those that experience them do not understand them or know what it is they are experiencing.

How can this be possible?

Ether, the ether is a place, a living space for the opposite of matter, and it creates a spirit of its own. With evolution and the intent of the great magical being, every volcanic rock has its master in the ether. The sea is owned by the great water sprite you call Neptune. There is a giant for each and each exists in a plane you do not see or hear only experience, their guardianship on the land and sea and the evidence in matter of their brutality, for instance when man dumps oil or waste into the sea and land. The effect it has on their being and their family, their offspring, their nature affects you all.

The snow giants exist, but not in the shape of man or animal, an energy of snow crystal, the patterns and shapes in the higher existence, an energy of light and water crystals. If there is snow, there is heat too. All weather patterns have its higher existence or an etheric equivalent.

What to believe and what not to believe?

It does not matter. It is and therefore will be, whether you believe or not. It is not about man's belief; it is about man's respect for where he lives and to live alongside the higher elemental plane with belief that he is part of the care required for the planet and is being guided by the higher elemental plane as much as he is guided intuitively and spiritually.

You are not separate from what the eye cannot see or the mind believe. You are part of the weather on Earth whilst in the body. There is a spirit of Earth; the elemental plane exists to harness this and act as a conduit between living creatures on Earth and the spiritual plane.

Rain, The Water

The pleasure of rain is to feed the plant life and give you all water, a vital ingredient you all need. The rain can come in many forms and different amounts in variety across the world, but it sustains you all and like the Sun that gives heat, rain can give you both, heat and cold, and either way, it can be pleasurable or miserable depending on many factors, such as wind and other weather factors that change the rain into sleet, hail or snow and you have to adapt to each and live with each; you cannot get rid of the weather, but you can contribute to its action on Earth and work with the consciousness of the weather.

It seems so unimaginable that the weather has an effect on you and your health, your mind, and your consciousness, but it does. You are wrapped in the earthly vibrations and you are made of water and your cells respond to the weather and give out signals and work with the vibrations of the earth, so if you are disturbed by a violent force on mass then the earth will respond. The integration is there, the facts unseen, but the evidence is always laid out before you when storms and tropical weather disrupt.

Fortunately, you think your scientific claims can rationalise the disturbance and turbulence, and you can justify the catastrophes and disruptions. It is not all bad, some is good, and some is great as when the positivity of your vibrations fills the air, the earth responds and nature's harmony, the spirits of the air and weather, collaborate and create. It goes on without your awareness and those that monitor the weather, of course, only see one perspective, their own and their knowledge, which is one part of the equation. The unseen, the integrations, is far greater at work than you know.

Can you measure this, judge this and see this?

No, but being aware and feeling this is what the Earth needs to grow and be nurtured, to sustain you all.

The rain is an essential part of life. We know if there wasn't any water, there would not be you, the body. Therefore, do you know what you need for your spirit to exist within the body?

Water also, the cells that hold your spirit cannot live without water and your spirit is held within your cells like ropes to the earth, it ties your spirit to the ground. Your spirit needs cleansed like your body, nourished like your body, and rejuvenated like your body. The two work together, body and spirit exist as one on Earth. Taking care of your spirit only or body only does not exist. You are always taking care of your spirit with what you eat, think, drink, and nourish your body with or feel or wear, or exercise. Absolutely everything counts, including the essential weather, the rain.

Live in the rain, be part of the rain, speak to the rain, acknowledge the rain, and love your rain, it is you.

The Wind Giants

Gentle breezes in the air are special and healing and clearing the vibration softly of the planet and you. The air nymphs are different from the wind giants that exist. The accumulation of wind giants over the years has come into existence in a ferocious way against the land and man. They are strong giants, determined creatures to clear away the harm of pollution and all that exist in their way. There have always been wind giants, but they have existed to heal and progress the planet, which they still do. Think of it as one of their functions, but they now have an additional function to clear the air of chemicals, smog, dirt and fumes, and telepathic air waves that they can no longer sustain. The ecological balance is becoming out of balance and the sickliness in the air is affecting you all, even the gentle nymphs that love to play on the winds breezes and gentle air flow.

It all seems like a fairy tale and unimaginable to the working mind, but see it from Spirit's perspective where you know nothing of the true life of Spirit, only experiencing one side of Spirit from a limited view on Earth. The untold beauty and magnificence of the Spirit world is far beyond your imagination and only those of the highest spiritual gifts can glimpse its truest existence. Those that have been to Spirit and back only remember the tiniest percentage of the world with a slightly distorted memory and even if they believe they have the clearest memory, it is still distorted from where you are in the third dimension. Imagine trying to look at the night sky through the weakest of binoculars and only seeing one perspective, one viewpoint, and the smallest view, squinting in the distance. But there have been exemptions to those that can draw, paint, and visualise the images imprinted on man's mind by the Elemental world and the Spirit world. William Blake, who you (the writer) know of, painted the picture of the other worlds we presented to him.

The glimpses that you all capture of the spiritual worlds should be as glimpses, so you can live in harmony with the Earth. It is not contradictory to be aware and work with the world of Spirit and the elementals. This is wonderful work you (the writer) and many others do, it is your bodies homeland and you must nurture your body with the Earth and let the world of Spirit and the elementals help you, so all can grow in the light and harmony and the destructive nature of your beings can lessen and not harm the planet and its creatures. This is the biggest lesson of all, for all of you on Earth, whether you do this unknowingly or knowingly.

The wind giants exist to provide good in the world. They help the planet immensely and need to be respected. They gather strength from man and help man in many situations. More importantly, they help and work with the Earth. Do not fear the wind or its power. Honour and respect the wind. Acknowledge its strength and let it clear your minds of unhealthy thoughts, destructive behaviour and let the wind sing and whistle through your beings.

The Firey Sprites

The elementals, for each of the elements of the Earth, there are far more types of elementals than we are covering in this book. Your awareness of the elemental world is my main aim, to bring the elementals to your group and more, this is my wish. Wishes, what a beautiful word and belief. To wish, but that is the nature of the elementals, to wish, to work with you in dreams and help you on your path, to bring about wishes. They work with those who want to work with them too, especially those within the arts, or have latent talents yet to emerge within the arts.

What is the purpose and how does this relate to the fire elementals?

Fire provides warmth, heat, and destroys materials. The fiery sprites that are with you (the writer) are those that are of nature, providing light in the dark, warmth to the other fairies. They glow and dance like flames in your fire. They are bright and are made of the fire elemental. They burn, but do not destroy. There are different kinds of fire elementals on the planet and different groups. The firey sprites can be seen as tiny orange dots in the air.

The range of elementals is vast and your awareness is all that is needed; to trust you are working with them and let them sprinkle their light around you to bring a brightness, uplift your spirit and clearing, the flame of life. Their spark is the spark of the creator. Do not upset the fire elemental, as it has the temperament of the fire and you can spark more than joy. Be respectful to the fiery sprite, and they will respect you.

I bring you a taste of the elemental world within my words, to show you there is far more life on the planet than just what the human eye can see. You have all heard the stories and the tales, and the literature is rich with many tales and truths of the elemental world. It exists, it is, and it is a part of the human Earth world. As you grow with nature to love your Earth, they will present themselves to you, work with you and inspire you with your work.

CHAPTER THREE
The Stars and Planets of Earth

The Stars and Planets

Listening to the stars isn't something you would think of doing, you like to look and see the visual beauty of the twinkling and moving stars in the night sky. But we ask you to listen as only looking reduces the experience.

What experience is this?

It is the sound of the night sky. The Earth resonates and sends out signals emitting a sound, and so do other planets. They are in tune with each other and resonate at different pitches. Like music, they have their harmony and vibrate bouncing off each other's signals. There is sound in the night sky. You have to develop your ears to attune to the Earth's peace, then the Earth's hum, and then the Earth's tune. This is a vague synopsis of what is really happening and how to attune yourself to the vibrations of the Earth, so you can hear the other stars and planets.

Sending out a conscious effort into the Universe is a vibration in itself and will be picked up. Every thought and action are living and either dissipates or stands up, depending on the strength of the signal. So, with determination and clarity, a thought, not a desire, a clear transparent thought can be picked up and responded to, so you can be helped to listen, to hear the night's tune. Not the earthly sounds of the night sky, the Earth itself, and the response from above your head, although it is all around you. The druids and others knew how to respond to the tune of the Earth and the planets. It was their way, and they could hear more than Earth's speak. Connecting with your planet is a special gift. No tools are required, just the willingness to hear, the time to devote to stand and listen and your ears attuned to spirit, first and foremost, repeating the practice and learning the discipline to hear.

You must first place yourself somewhere undisturbed and in a quiet spot of nature with no cars or earthly disturbances. Take your mind to your physical ears, feel the outer ears to the inner ears. Sit quietly and feel the spiritual ears, behind and below your physical ears, resonate with the Earth. Listen.

When you are feeling quiet, use your stillness to hear the sounds around you, then quieten your earthly senses and physical noise and the spiritual senses to hear the night sky. Give it time as the ears adjust and practice listening for the hum of the Earth, then the tune of the Earth. Expand your listening to the night sky and hear the song of space.

The Sun

A living being that fires up Earth, the two working in harmony, living side by side.

So, can anyone exist within the Sun? Is the energy of the Sun more untapped than we know? Does the Sun have a higher existence or is it just a gas ball of light and fire burning so brightly that anything that upsets the equilibrium of the Sun will extinguish you all, including the planet, so many unanswered questions?

The Sun is a giver of life, worshiped throughout history providing warmth, nourishment, light, life and death, direction, and travel. The Sun is essential for life and guidance. It guides Earth, leads her through space, the empty space?

No, the full space of life. It is full of life and existence in space. You just can't see it, or feel it, or know as it is hidden from your perspective. Your eyes do not have the capacity to see all in the Universe. But you can glimpse, and those that have been given the unnatural sight of God, can see and even hear the deep echoing in space and sounds unknown to your ears. Vocal sounds as if they are suspended in space, but the drawn-out voices are delayed in time, reaching your ears like a recording slowed down many times, so that all you hear is a deep resonance like a bear calling out to its companions.

Therefore, the Sun is guiding others, too, and a source of energy for more than the planet Earth. But for the purpose of this book, we tell you to work with the Sun, not to worship it like an idol; to work with its energy in giving your vital organs life, feeding, and nourishing your body, bringing well-being to your physical. It also brings light and life to your spiritual self. It cleanses, fills you up with energy, brightens your house, and clears the energetic air waves that have become clogged with the unwanted vibrations of others, environments, and materials. It refreshes your soul, relaxes the body, and the overall well-being is much needed to bring you energy and renewal.

Stand in the Sun and feel its warmth regardless of the temperature. Stand in its warmth and absorb the rays into your energy field. Let it fire up the spiritual and feed the soul. Let it speak to you and guide each of you throughout the day. The focus on the Sun's energy helps you clear the mind and bring in maybe one or two thoughts that need to rise to the surface that help you progress throughout your day or progress in the spiritual mind.

The Sun, always there forever lighting up your world and continually burning bright to bring heat and warmth. But is it more than a gas ball in the sky?

It is a compass in the world of space like a lighthouse for those that travel throughout the air and beyond, a pointer for direction and travel.

For you on Earth, soak up its rays to heal, cleanse your energy and feed your spirit within, to harness a clear picture, to feel nourished and enlivened, to regain strength for the physical body as well as the spiritual body. Let the Sun shine into your heart to clear out old energy, renew your thinking, and brighten your life.

It is important to bring balance to everything in your life, and knowing when you have had the right amount to replenish is a siren to stop so you do not burn. The Sun's rays penetrate the Earth's skies more easily than ever before and the harm is damaging to your physical body.

Carry the energy of the Sun's rays for good.

The Moon

The Moon has a special and unique bond with Mother Earth, working in harmony together. Its gravitational pull affects you all. The energy of the Moon works with the energy of the Earth, and the Sun dominates and leads the merry dance.

So, the three work together?

No, the nine work together connected to the twelve that work together, along with the fifteen that work together. Planets connect and interconnect, but the most obvious to you are the Earth, Sun, and the Moon.

The scientists know a lot about the Moon and now easily study the Moon. Pictures, along with studies, show the Moon is highly significant to you all. The Moon is like a shining star on the planet lighting up your world at night. Yet, only a few of you follow the true energy of the Moon. Just as few of you connect with the earth to ground your energy, nurture the earth, and listen to the earth, the healing energy of the Moon is rarely used knowingly by man. Yet, the elementals depend greatly upon its energy for inspiration, healing, and rejuvenation. The Moon brings life to their bodies and fills their spirits with healing energy. It is revitalising and nourishing. The Moon speaks to them and they dance in its rays, the healing beams of the Moon. The more developed your spiritual self, the more easily you connect with the magic of the Moon. You can feel the energy enhancing your human nature, cleansing, and healing, and easily revitalising your body forms as there are several layers to the human form.

When you stand in the light of the full Moon, the bond is strong and just as we ask you to absorb sunlight for your health and spirit; the moonlight is needed especially for the mental mind. The aura fills up with unwanted thoughts, clutters and requires detoxing more so than before with the streams of mental stimulation you receive, to decrease the over activity balance your mind in the Moon. Declutter and empty unwanted thoughts. The Moon's energy is continually powering the Earth; let it charge your energies. Like electricity, it is a powerful current. Work with the Moon in the different phases, get to know your Moon. Open your spiritual self to the energy of the Moon and make the time to feel the Moon's energy.

Those that work with tools to enhance the spiritual self, such as physical stones, crystals, tarot cards, candles are all materials that have come from the earth and bathed in the light of the Moon and the stars and the Sun. Place them in the full moonlight to enhance their energies, fill their auras with this misunderstood energy. It will cleanse them of old energy that stagnates around them. Your thought-forms stick to materials, so does happy or negative energy, so ensure the energy is bright, clean, and happy. It affects you all. Everything is energy, so use the power of the Moon.

When the sky is dark, wherever you are, as you know the Moon is there, is the power less?

Yes, it is resting; the Moon sleeps without Sun, as you do, but the spirit of the Moon is working as you do. You are all connected.

The essential ingredients of life, food, and water require the energy of the Moon for revitalisation and growth. Put plant food in the full Moon and absorb its nutrients at its fullest potential to heal the inner organs of the body. Drink water that has absorbed the light of the full Moon and you will feel invigorated. Ensure your utensils are clay or stone, unpolished and clean when working this way with the Moon.

Stand in the energy of the Moon and receive its light. The night light will energise your spiritual self and restore your body if penetrated deeply enough. Let the moonbeams into your aura and soak up the rays. Feel what the elementals feel and let the joy of life run through your body like a current, nature's electricity. Connect with the earth and absorb its magnetic field with your own to transform you. Let the energy soak into your being to feel more alive and vibrant, desensitised from the electronic light, demagnetised from your earthly home, and magnetised with the earth.

There is a difference, changing your energy from the use of unnatural materials and the overuse of man-made electricity and fumes in the home to the natural substance that you are made from of the earth. It will calm and reduce hyperactivity in your body.

The Moon keeps the Earth energised and, therefore; it plays an important part in energising you. Reach out to the Moon, let it heal you.

The Earth

Do you know the Earth is a living being sharing the same experiences as you?

Everything you do and say vibrates into the Earth, leaves an imprint, and resonates for many years after you have left. Therefore, if you are a light being, you should understand why your light is important to heal the Earth and projecting your light out upon her keeps the Earth in a vibration of renewal and growth. You are placed on Earth to love the planet, enjoy her abundance, and nurture her life. But this is not so, and we require more of you to expand your consciousness and light to restore the living being, Earth.

If your hands hold one branch with love, it runs deep into the tree and throughout the soil. It sounds like a made-up story, but your scientists know this, they know man's imprint on the land. It is measured, counted, and documented.

Your body absorbs all your thoughts and actions. Everything that has been mentally, physically, and spiritually lived lives in your cells, so when you bury your body deep in the Earth, you bury the ideas, the feelings, the life of the human being that existed on Earth. It dissipates over time and absorbs into the soil. But not only is every action recorded in the great halls of life, it is left behind on Earth, which is why it affects the elementals. They absorb and work with humans' feelings and thoughts. They are there to help, not hinder. So, the more of you that become out of balance, the more of you feel unwell, and the sickness spreads through your bodies mentally, physically, and emotionally.

To stop the circle of sickness, the cleansing and purifying of the body needs to take place and this will in turn heal the mind and then when you dig your ditch for your body, it will heal the Earth. If you burn your body, it has the same reaction in the air, the smoke carries the messages of you in the airwaves and the ashes stay for a time with the Earth. What a grim topic you may think this is, but would you not like to leave your body healed in love to replant within the Earth, or if you desire to fly with the elementals and sprinkle the harmony of you over the land? What a beautiful thought to prepare for your departure from the Earth, something you all face, but human misery can create disharmony amongst you and the land.

The Earth is also a great and knowing being that has many ways to cleanse itself and heal itself. The Earth also has a great form of communication amongst its plant and animal life. It is a very special place, the Earth, and where you have built monolithic cities, the Earth suffers.

The Earth is still the playground for your learning, and the diversity is broad with a divide that is widening between those that understand and those that do not, for many reasons.

So, let us gather in light to generate healing for the Earth, let us project magical thoughts of green entering the cities, and let us take control of our well-being spiritually, emotionally, and physically. Let us help those that need the light and let us be a nation of light. For this is not a fantasy, all is connected, counted, recorded, and blessed with the ribbon of life, the light that made you all and is.

CHAPTER FOUR

Life on Earth

The Animal Kingdom

The variety in the animal kingdom has changed over the many years of Earth's existence and many were brought to the planet and many evolved with the planet. But in the main, they are made of Spirit and exist in the spiritual world as well as the physical world. Some are like the nature spirits and go back to the creator to be reborn either individually or as a part of another energy group, such as birds or ants or snakes. But when they become your pets, they become a part of you and take on a persona and individual form that moves them forward in their spiritual growth.

Man can help the animals do this, but to treat animals as pets, to be nurtured, loved, and gain strength in the world, they depend on your care, goodwill, and your trust. On the whole, man loves his pets and some are better at looking after animals than others. The role of the animal brings man many lessons to learn, to care, look after others, discipline oneself as well as the animal. Healing becomes a large part of the nurturing as animals absorb man's energy and will uplift their nature and take the negative away from man and corrupt their own physical body in an attempt to please, heal and cure the master. It is natural for animals to heal; they are healing beings.

From the lion to the tiger, bear, eagle and dolphin and whale, the mighty leaders are of great significance in your world and inhabit your world to balance the Earth, its food chain, its seasons and land, sea, and air. Their energy is vital for the Earth, the soil, the sea, the atmosphere and deep within the land, the insects, the moving creatures of the night. All play a part in the balance of Earth's nature. But if man continues to ruin the soil, the air, the landscape then the habitats of the animals are ruined and they can no longer exist to contribute to your existence and look after the plantation, the food chain, the soil, the oceans, and rivers. Animals know animals, but humans have yet to know humans. Your instinct has disappeared to work as a flock, a group, a tribe alongside the animal kingdom.

So, the Earth works overtime in an attempt to heal herself and the existence on the surface of her planet.

Animals are guides to humans, whether as pets or living in the wild, but there are animals that crossover as neither pet nor wild, but as man's food, ill-treated and suffering beyond sanity, living insanely that their pain and fear is splitting the world in two and more. Do not live in ignorance, the slaughter and ill-treatment of animals is a dark world, so when man eats their meat and skin, they take on the persona of the deliverer of the slaughter, the energy of the killer, the energy of the animals living in fear, trepidation, sickness, and insane with pain. This has always been so, but man has not grown and desires meat and flesh that has been insanely treated and wonders why he is sick or feels unwell.

All is connected on Earth, every living creature speaks, whether individual or in a group, you are all together for a purpose, to move forward. In my time, I did not eat meat. I understand the language of animals and respected all creatures great and small and lived happily eating seeds, nuts, berries, flowers, and fruits. Vegetables dug from the earth growing naturally, that were rich in nutrients and I understood fish swimming together hydrating the rivers and eating the grubs and plants of the water, but I did not eat the fish as I understood their purpose and to me, they were my friends. There is a manner to eating fish and animals, but this has been lost as you do not know how to speak to the animal kingdom, and those that do, can be counted on two hands. I do not talk of the pet communicators; I talk of the human guides of animals purposefully on your planet to show you the true nature of animals. It is mainly viewed as entertainment and ignored by most, you try, the human race is trying to eradicate the insane slaughter and maltreatment of animals, but failing miserably as it still exists in large numbers.

So, how can my past help you now?

Talk to the animals in spirit as there are so many of you that have developed your spirituality and meditate and see the animal guides and know the animal guides and are starting to understand the animals of the Spirit world, that they can help you move forward with the animals of the physical world. The communication will broaden, understand their lessons they bring and their language they speak. To free all animals from the food chain will take a long time, to stop the insane treatment of the animals can be done quickly, let the desire bring in the new energy for animals to be freed from a life of purgatory and be treated on Earth as God's creatures.

Animals are man's saviour, what does this mean?

Animals can help man grow to become pure in themselves. If you can understand the life and nature of an animal, you can understand yourself. Do not idolise animals, revere them, and for the lion to exist naturally, their land must return, where man does not encroach upon their existence, but overlooks their care. Many animals have lost their homes and their true nature taken away from them; many animals need help. Look to the communities and societies that care for the birds and animals, be prepared to help those that need your help. Talk to the animals, be guided by your spiritual guides to help those in need. Those can be one, a few or many, all will be counted.

Life on Earth is treasure to the spirit, but when you are on Earth, you see more than you desire and the life of one animal can impact greatly on your journey.

What is the difference between an individual animal and an individual human?

There are many differences in the earthly nature of animals and humans, but none in Spirit. Take care of your animals that need the human race to provide, nurture and care. Humans are creating a beastly world far more dangerous than your wildest animals can create on Earth. Animals live on the planet for humanity to learn to live with nature.

If you believe they are food, then they are food. If you believe they are pets, then they are companions. If you believe in their truest nature, then you know they are spirit, just as you are.

The Sea World

Within the sea you see a beautiful existence of fish and marine life and the large mammals that are centuries old, with age old wisdom of the Spirit world and Earth world. If only they could communicate to you the way of life as it has been and is and will be, but you continue to destroy the seas with plastic and pollution, so it is now killing your mammals and fish and plant life in the sea. This waters down to the rivers polluting streams and oceans and waterways and lakes and any pool of water, whether hidden beneath the ground or sitting on land.

This has greatly affected the elemental world of the sea, but the visions of mermaids, the stories of living sea life deep in the earth that you have never encountered and the dancing elemental sea life, all has existed and still continues to do so, but under smaller spaces, under duress and hidden away from man as they are not ready to encounter any more sorrow from the human that pollutes their sea.

I cannot tell you what the toxic harm has done to your own life, I am not here to judge or throw further guilt upon you all; I am here as a request on behalf of the Spirit world and the new humans to be born into your world, to request that you all try and commit to a cleaner way of life. We know you feel you are fighting the economic situation, the wars, the terror, and the hardship of day to day living, but not all and if you can lead by example it will spread, the consciousness, the awareness will spread amongst you all that it will eventually create a full stop, as you will not be able to drink your water and you all require water to live.

The joy of the elemental world within the sea does and still exists, and helps many of you lost at sea or at sea. Amongst the edges of rivers, canals and lakes, lochs and sea pools are many little creatures that are ignited by sand and sea, rock, and shells, and much more. But again, your beaches are riddled with waste that drives the little creatures away and the change in your world has affected the harmony amongst the sea life and land life.

To bring hope, work with your energy by the sea and water. Let the energy of water heal you, and your light will be recognised by those who live out of view, within the sea. They will naturally react to your human energy and vibration of healing light and blessings will be created and they can improve the sea and inspire you how to improve your energy with the sea.

The sea is a special place, and the variety of oceans brings a variety of sea elementals. Send out light across the sea, be the lighthouse to attract the sea elementals to connect and work with you to heal the waters of Earth.

The Human Race

Where is the human race heading? With all the technology and spiritual growth, is the Earth's world any better for the human race?

Yes, and no, the human race is killing the Earth's world as well as loving the Earth. The human race is living amazing lives as well as unsavoury and uncomfortable lives. The difference is wide and the difference is unsatisfactory.

We would like the human race to develop the Earth world into a place of beauty for animals, all creatures and a place of learning, a global community spirit, but the toxic energy through chemicals and man-made products is too rife and the poor are very poor.

Is it always meant to be like this on Earth? Is it always going to be like this on Earth?

The despondency felt by so many, and even in the delivery of these words, makes it seem impossible and hopeless.

But we want to give you hope, encouragement, and fuel for the growth of the human race as a whole. There will be a shift and a divide and the choice will change on Earth, whether you come for a dense experience or an enlightened experience. The human race as a whole is changing drastically and you are all making the decision every day to either grow or decline.

The huge shift in spiritual consciousness has prepared Earth for a higher vibratory playground and Earth itself will change. The frequency of her vibrations is quickening. The light on the Earth world from many of you is making a marked difference, but the light must spread to those that are suffering in the dark, alone, terrified, and struggling to grow in the circumstances they have chosen or find themselves, either through unfortunate decisions, or hindrances, or temptation.

Man has become very selfish looking at his own needs and desires and concentrating on his way of life. We are not saying every person is like this; we are saying the majority of you have become so focused on who you are and what you do and at this time of the distorted view through global communication amongst you; it is very much needed to send light to one other human that is suffering in some way that will help the human race as a whole. Spread the light amongst you all to see the changes with the Earth world.

Do not mix this up with helping yourself and concentrating on your growth, as this is highly important. It is balance you seek and the balance has tipped amongst many of you to be only thinking of yourself.

To put these words into context, we know that many of you send light, give out love, and show great acts of kindness. Therefore, enhance your acts of kindness, light, and love, so others can see your light and love. Lead by example to show the many that do not know how to behave with compassion. We say this as the new souls that come to Earth at this time, in the burst of spiritual consciousness and growth of human communication, need your wisdom and guidance to help them through the torrent of information thrown at them, that they can easily lose their way unnecessarily. It is not all wrong or right; it is to help the growth of human consciousness.

Seeing the Elementals

Rainbow, colours, magnetic clouds of light, spectacular auroras are all a result, a conclusion of weather patterns, and a spectacle for the eye. Sheer patterns of beauty that you can see made visible by the earth's elements and conditions. So, replicate that more than ten thousand times and you have the elemental world living in sheer beauty and delight that you cannot see, as it lies just beyond the human eye. They will show themselves if you work honestly, with complete respect to not harm them, the earth or any of the Creator's creatures, and they will show you who they are, for you to see visibly with the human eye. It is easier for them to show you with the inner eye, as it is the spiritual vibration in which they live. With the right conditions, you can see the elementals twinkling at night, colourful by day and in joy you will see them.

If more of you can practice raising your vibrations, not only for your own benefit, but for the benefit of the elemental realm, so they can begin to work with more of you. To inspire, to encourage, to enhance your lives, improve your awareness of working with the Earth. They are ready as a team, as a nation, as a realm in harmony to work more in harmony with the human to protect the Earth world from disasters and destruction on a huge scale. It not only affects your homes when mountains collapse, but theirs too. Remember the encouragement, not the disaster, remember the fascination and wonder they bring, not the doom and misery of past mistakes that may not be yours. Do not point any finger, just be in the spirit of nature and the nature spirits will be with you.

Pot those plants in your house, do not forget them, nurture them for the fairies and elementals to swing by your homes and bring inspiration and joy to you all.

What you bring to them is significant too, your ability to create whatever you want within your range of talents is beyond them, nigh on impossible. They are given their one function, albeit in purity, and abide by it like a spiritual law that cannot be broken. It is, for they fully enjoy what they do and live for what they do. They can help you with your creations and enjoy watching you at work and encouraging you to paint, draw, write, sing, dance, play, play music, create music, create, create, create. They are Mother Earth's beautiful creation.

Do not be disappointed if the elemental realm stays hidden for a while or longer from your view. One day I guarantee you will see the Earthly realm through renewed eyes and the delight and wonder will be more than magical. Filmmakers, artists, painters have all been inspired and, through the pictorial world, you touch just how magnificent they are; do not doubt when someone paints or sketches their version of an elemental. The elemental world is colourful with an abundance of variety and it is up to the human to believe, to know they exist.

Your world will expand with their world and your growth will expand as they do. It is all within the divine making and the growth will be seen in the new lands that you are inspired to produce, new earth friendly houses, materials and communities of inspired higher nature living, where animals can roam free and be part of the community. All will be taken care of; the future is there and the possibilities are numerous and parts of the Earth will survive in a higher vibration. For now, take care of where you are and what you do, be honest and true, respect all that is and live your best life with Mother Nature.

Those that can see the elemental world do not sit back and view for pleasure, they come to ask for your help. Let them inspire you to help them.

Ask your spiritual guide, what can I do for the elemental world? What is it I have to give back not only for humanity, but for the world I know that is working hard for Mother Earth?

We thank you from the Spirit world as we know who will take up this task and we are waiting for you, ready to work with you.

Those that are willing to help, and have not seen any signs of the elemental world, we know this too and you will be taken on a journey that will uncover many inspirations. Give it time, let it flower, for the flower fairies love to help those that need their help and will help you too; flowers are man's beautiful reflection of his own spiritual nature. Breathe in their essence, it is part of you.

CHAPTER FIVE

Living Your Magic on Earth

The Magic of Life

Finding your magic inside of you is easy, but you cannot find it when you look so hard.

Is it something you have to practice every day, or is it something you have to think about? What is the magic of life? What is the existence of an 'other worldly' creation on Earth?

Magic exists in the heart of all creation. It seems so remote to look at this world with so much disaster and chaos and ignorance to think there is magic amongst you all and within your beings, but there is and the magic is life itself. But most of you cannot see it, the colours in your aura, what you attract with words and action, the pulsing heartbeat of you magnetically transmitting out to the world and above. The spirit of you is pure magic, vibrating at a frequency that is golden and light, sparkling in sunshine, bathed in love and so bright it would blind you if you could see the true light on Earth.

So, to live in the light is the magic, to sweep away dark thoughts, dark matter and not entertain the cruelties and suffering is misleading too as your light is needed in these very places, so the light of higher beings and the celestial greatness can enter into the spaces of grim and gloom to brighten the being that needs it the most.

Light and dark are the two opposites in this world, Earth, and they each play a significant part. The magic of light is the magic of this world I communicate to you now. But do not entertain yourself or create actions in the dark, this is not your (the writer) path and nor the path of many, but many learn through lessons of darkness, but the existence of the magic of creation lies in the light. Light is key to creating a magical life.

What is magic? The appearance of something that has not been created and exists only in your imagination?

No, magic is life and about how you embrace life and use the skills given to you from the onset of birth. Every man's direction is different and not one man has travelled the same path, but each of you requires the light to lead your way. You are the light and you are the way. It is determination that leads some men and fear that drives others, but this is not magical.

Magic is following your intuition and being led by the heart. You may think everyone knows this, but not everyone does this and not everyone knows this within themselves. Some men force their magic aggressively and make things happen with intention of willpower, but this is not the magic power we are discussing. It is the magic of your spiritual team, the helpers that work behind the scenes to help you go through doors, heal you, lead you to open new doors and inspire you to act differently and go beyond your fear and worries. You are all gently led to greater good of yourselves and others, but the will is strong and sometimes misled and sometimes misheard and for some drowned out by mental patterns that have become habit or misguided.

Give up the mind each day to let in the divine inspiration, bring in the heavenly vibrations. Not all of you are ready for this and do not believe this, but this book is intended for those that want to practice or learn the way of the magic of life. Learning about yourself is an important step and each man's version of a magical life is unique and different. Yet, working with a higher consciousness brings responsibility and duty to your spirit and to yourself as you have opened a door that leads you further along the enlightened path.

Learning to meditate or quiet the mind, being peaceful in nature or one with your own spirit is of importance to create a life of magic. The mind needs rest and recuperation, refuelled with its divine creator and your spirit needs 'air time' to lead you in the direction of your true intention, to remind you of your path and your will to be realigned to the will of your spirit, the nature of One.

Breathe in light and give out love throughout your portals, the chakras and reenergise the being of you. Connect to a higher force of good, positivity and energy that is YOU.

Managing Time

What is time? A man-made effort, a God given ruler and measurement?

It is an evolution of the planet Earth. The dimension of time gives you a playground to learn in order and with discipline. It is a measurement that rules your lives and gives you focus and every living thing in existence in your realm is measured, counted, blessed, and learning to be an evolution of God, the creator, the energy that binds you all to divinity and beyond.

How to use time wisely and to beguile time and to create the magic of time is to connect to the higher energy of all that exists. Start with yourself and the rest will follow. It is when you disconnect from your own higher being or the all of you that you fail and feel miserable when things go wrong or you misinterpret an action. The swings of moods affect your time. Controlling your emotions helps you bide your time and work in alignment with your growth and magnificence. Wasting time on useless actions or drivel is a forgotten time, but useful action even rest, and healing when it is most needed creates energy that will help you build and grow, move forward in your expansion, and build worlds within your world.

Time is precious to man and spending your time wisely is the lesson well learnt. Following your intuition to use your time wisely is the key to knowing what to do. But when other lives impact on your own and take you away from your purpose or your path, then you weave a new path within a path.

Your task is to know if the impact is on your true path? The test, the lesson, how to deal with the impact, and how to know what to do next?

For example, if you see a deer running through the woods chasing something you cannot see, but are intrigued and want to follow the deer.

Will this take you somewhere you have never been and will this enhance your experience on Earth? Will this take you somewhere that is dangerous or will this take you somewhere you are needed?

Every moment is a decision using your higher guidance, an intuition you have been given and following every step of your life can create confusion in your being and nonsense in your head making a lot of people unwell and the clearing out of mental thought patterns, confusions, disturbance to your being is necessary to keep the electromagnetic waves of your being clear and precise with your higher energy, the soul of you, so you can hear your radar and you can follow and act upon your own radar.

Training your ears and heart to work as companions is of the utmost importance. Some have perfected this, some are working on this, some are selfish and can easily do this and some just don't know as their circumstances dictate the action they find themselves surrounded by. Calling upon your higher self and the energy of spirit, which constantly surrounds everyone in the Earth world, helps you to follow your true path.

Lessons go hand in hand with time, some have come with tough lessons to overcome and grow intensely and some have easier lessons and others know nothing of their lessons not ready to work with their higher, but are here to enjoy and be a part of the Earth world experience. Do not be side-tracked by their so-called luck, their path is made easier for the new souls to handle the Earth world and there are souls that have asked for an easier experience to learn fewer lessons even just one or two as their previous lives have been filled with sorrow, hardship and hurt to a degree you cannot understand. But God wants them to heal and share their light, as everyone is the light, made of light, and exists in the light. Time is a tool and a blessing.

Time is a concept, an illusion, but very real whilst living on Earth in the third dimension. You can slip in and out of time with the spiritual forces at work and when you connect to Spirit, time does not exist. Time is a true blessing and curse for some. Make the most of your time on Earth, every living moment counts, is counted, and adds up or takes away; either way your time is precious, a commodity that always requires your attention.

Living in the now is powerful, loving who you are is powerful, creating the potential of you towards the future is more powerful, learning, accepting, and loving the past to grow is extremely powerful. Make the most of time, every part of time is truly a blessing on Earth, this is why your spirit came to Earth, to experience living and learning in time.

Respecting Yourself

My life led me to respect myself, which I did not as a young man. I was led astray and it threw me into madness, and I needed the wilderness to tame my mind and bring forward the fruition of my magic within me. It was my crazy mind that cleared and brought forth the beauty of other worlds into my worlds that created calm, peace and a loving respect of life that healed my whole being. I loved Earth and still do. I connect to Earth through you, the writer, and many of you to help with the development of nurturing the Earth, respecting the Earth. It is highly important to respect yourself to grow in a lifetime on Earth.

As man is on many different levels, many different journeys and the diversity is at an all-time high, learning to know yourself and respect yourself has become more important in this time living on Earth.

Why?

Because you are governed by a power that wants to control everything you do, say, behave, and eat. You may think this has always been so, no, this has not. You are all a number, address and connected by the electronic communication and served food from an electronic device, programmed to think, behave, and act in a manner the few desires, holding the key to your device.

Step aside and learn to know you and respect you, your actions so that when you use the power of those holding the key to the global world, you can use it for giving not feeding yourself with a consciousness of others. Use the device as a library of knowledge for learning, not a library of information to tempt, corrupt and mislead. Finding your own power is practising your art of listening to you.

Man has made himself sick with the world of what everyone else is doing, what are you doing? How are you contributing to the energy of a new world that speaks of higher vibrations, frequencies that are God felt, a purpose to give and share your gifts?

In my day, when I met a man or woman or child that needed conversation, help, healing, play or information, we talked. There was no other way than to use the communication of the tongue and act with the body and interact with body language, using the power of the senses. Now, certain senses are weakening, and others are growing. It is good you have new communication for the good it does, but man must stay true to himself and steer away from the electronic light to return to his own electronic energy, the magical power within your bones, flesh, and blood, sending signals out into the world and communicating with others. You are the transmitter and the receiver; an animal knows nothing of this through the electronic light; you need to interact with animals to communicate. Man must learn to respect himself and interact with humans to be human through the physical energy.

Being on one's own is of importance too, to get to know oneself and to feel you, to hear you and to be you. Not all can do this and this is the diversity, this is the different levels. But for those who want to know themselves, time with you is a great healer, time and space with your own energy helps you interact at your best with other humans. Respect you to know you.

My life as a magician is incorrect, but my being as a magician of Spirit is correct. I developed my powers of spirituality that can create energy of a higher degree. Begin with taking time out to be you, find out who you are and let the magic of you begin to unfold. To be a master, you must first master you. Take each step slowly, start with respect for you. Value what you have, love what you have and approve of who you are to respect you.

How to Clear Confusion

I was confused for a very long time with life, people, and circumstances. I did not know which path to tread and did not understand the ways and minds of people. The advice I received led me on different paths and I decided to be on my own early in my life to find me, the true path of me in my lifetime as Merdith. I knew to harness myself; I needed to be alone, to balance my true nature with nature that could show me how to be strong, intuitive, clear and a survivor. Then I became influential as I grew and knew more than myself. I knew how to be and I took control of my power and knowings. I protected them and let them lead me.

When your world becomes unclear, tangled and you feel the lack of clarity and knowing and despair begins to creep in, it is time to stop all actions and to restart with a different mindset and energy to bring in knowings and clarity.

It seems simple, but it is not easy to do when you want to shake up the world and make it happen, demand it happen and force it to happen. Using force can break something, making a demand can create a wrong action and trying to make it happen can be a wasted effort. It is deceiving when people who have succeeded say, 'I made it happen' when they should state 'I received a strong intuition and followed exactly the actions I knew to take, which created the results that made it feel like I made it happen'.

There is never 'I' it is always we, but it is you that must pick up the mantle when the intuition guides you, the knowings tap at your door. If you do not answer the door to opportunity, there will be another door and another knock and another way with another opportunity. Infinite ways with infinite possible outcomes and variations upon variations of opportunities for different times in your life, so flow when you know to go and stop when it feels like a block. Spend time on other areas in your life, let go and watch out for the surprise, the outcome coming to you.

Letting go is the key action for the confusion to clear and dissipate from your mind and out of your aura. Direction is an outcome already created in the mind of the Great Spirit. Pre-determined, pre-ordained, it is written already in the stars literally, you know what you have to do in the chosen lifetime, you pack up your bags from Spirit, get on the train to Earth and say, 'when I grow up, I'm going to do this as I know this is what I must do and I created the direction before I came to Earth'.

For those that do not grow up, the lessons are quick, short, and valid for their growth. For those that take on great burdens to overcome, there is a way, and letting in the way to be shown through instinct, intuition and guidance can be harder when the mental picture is blurred and confused. It is time to let go and finding what to let go of can be the most difficult part, along with letting go. Finding a focus to grasp onto can help redirect your path to letting go and finding your truth.

So, where does it all seem to go wrong for some of you, when lives become unfulfilled, unhappy, turnings down paths that feel uncomfortable?

Sometimes the spirit in you is distracted by other people, actions, and outcomes, sometimes it eludes you of what you are pursuing and creating, sometimes it feels so uncomfortable that you give up on your path as the easy route has become the devil that tempted you. No matter what, each direction will lead back to your home in Spirit and you find a new direction with a new plan. It is all good.

Lessen the worry, the confusion, and let clarity be your aim, as this will bring the intuition you seek for the direction that will take you to your dreams.

Mother Earth offers all that you need to clear the confusion, bring peace to the mind, and help redirect you on your path. Find time in nature, it is essential, as it rebalances your energies, revitalises your spirit, nourishes, and replenishes you.

Existence

Existence to exist 'is'. You can not exist. You have been born, you have been bred, you have been, and you are 'all that is'. But in your earthly lives (and amongst others) you forget, and your growth can be halted and hindered by following the way of the world on Earth. The time dictates whether you can be who you truly are or whether you survive, maintain your presence on Earth with listening to the Earth, joining forces with the Earth and being with the Earth. This is of importance too many of you, and some try to ignore the Earth's offerings on their quest to be spiritual; their search to be of Spirit rather than of nature and Spirit.

So, I am here with you to pass on the magic of being both. The balance, the harmony you need between Earth and Spirit. How to let the Earth's magnetic nature serve you and be led by your higher nature simultaneously so that you balance all of who you truly are; this is a discipline many are unable to manage, and the disharmony creates an unhappy being.

We must serve you as well as you serve us, the Spirit world.

Why?

So, that we can all progress and move the world into expansion, so the Earth world is enlightened too, its vibrations raised and healed and as a result, the universal energy is raised too, simultaneously.

Is this nonsense?

No, truth and scientific facts are determining the truth, but not revealing the truth. Spiritual gurus of the highest order know the truth and have been before on Earth and the interaction of other beings from other celestial stars have visited to assist the Earth people to help the overall galaxy you live in.

Your dimension is one dimension, there are other dimensions and like rooms that you move through, we can move through the dimensions.

But like your postman delivering mail at the door, do you let them in, or do you say: 'thank you for the mail' and close the door, or do you follow the postman to look for more mail?

This simple analogy is all that it is, doorways leading to more doorways leading to places you have never been or discovered and we are trying to keep the portals managed, so that the discovery of your higher self does not delude you from your earthly self and you are helped to do both, raise the vibrations and pursue your earthly activities, day to day living and dreams of goals of who you would like to be, represent and deliver in this lifetime.

Complicated, it is not, but Earth people like to make it complicated, so the mystery can elude them and the blame can be attached to how difficult life is, which it is not. Following your heart is a big part of this, listening to your higher self, the spirit of you and your inner guidance, knowing which path to take, which decision to make, which will be fruitful, and which will be best for your spirit.

Beyond your comprehension?

Not really, it is within your grasp not to shut out the truth of you, and many have done this so they can cope, live and be in an earthy realm that seems so one-dimensional, but it is not. It is more than one dimension as it exists in the third dimension, with many doorways entering into other dimensions.

Is life a game?

No, a life is love and being in love and preparing for a greater love, to be one with love.

The brave that come to Earth corrupted, undisciplined, poor, in suffering environments, and unimaginable woe, play a great part in their own learning and teaching to those who have a need for compassion, love, or light. Until you unite the balance to bring in a world of peace and love on Earth, it cannot be, you must all help each other to be in the dimension you dream of, a higher dimension and this is the shift, the movement to progress the Earth world into a higher dimension, to enter nearer to the kingdom of God.

Why?

It must be, as you have started the movement, your consciousness has grown and your light beings need a place to grow beyond the Earthly portal. The richness now on your planet is proof of your growth. The disdain and cruelty and poverty, which has always been, grows too; managing the balance is important.

Existence is, therefore, live in your dimension with light and love. Know you are all loved, and all taken care of and be as one in spirit, but divided in unity on Earth. Let the higher energy of you and the Great Spirit in to your lives to lead you, guide you, and bring you all the ingredients you need to fulfil a lifetime on Earth in the most harmonious way.

The Days I Doubted

We all have days we doubt until we know so strongly within our being there is no doubt, no fear, no worry, and no stress, there only is, an energy that is there for each and every one residing within you, reminding you every day to believe in Him, the One, the Divine, the higher power of you that there only is and this is, is you.

His infinite and mighty power can light you up in seconds, can rearrange and reschedule your way with His trust and His energy. It is not hidden; it is in the heart, in your blood cells, bones and muscles, every cell has his signature written in to your being, you are encoded with the higher power, and like a battery cell it needs the positive and negative to ignite, to power up your engine. This is the way.

Controlling your negative energy, your darker moments, your fears, and doubts, is the whole point of you being on Earth, to control the fire that burns within you. Do not let the flames of joy, happiness, and good burn out or diminish, relight this fire inside of you, the way you know how, to be in nature is the best cure as your body needs the energy of nature to balance your mind, spirit, and body.

Why?

It has more of you in nature as you are in the human form. The spirit needs this earthly matter to cleanse you in bodily form. For your car to run well, it needs fuel that is clean, a simple analogy, but nature is your clean fuel. Connecting with nature is highly important when you are on the spiritual path of enlightenment, and even if you say you are not, it is still highly important to be with mother nature in whatever form, as you are all on the spiritual path at some level and striving for balance and seeking more of who you are in your lifetime on Earth.

How to take control?

Ask, put out the vibration of a request to your people that surround you in the spirit world and you will be guided to the answers, the people to guide you truly on the right and most wholesome path for you to lead. Do not expect the answers immediately, although this can happen, expect nothing, go about being you, as positive as you can, maybe in a minor way or doing as little as possible, even do nothing till you know the right action, but let the depressed mind disappear out of your being.

Be in thankfulness for what is right, what you have, what you can do and see. Be in appreciation of the changing moments and let them build within, as to eliminate suffering of the mind is a big task when it has gripped you for many years. The shedding has to take place and the rebuilding and rewiring and the recoding, so you are the programme of the Great Spirit and His intention is your intention, His will is your will and your power is His power. To be it, the great sorcerer of life is to know oneself inside out and action what you can with what you have been given, your talents, your gifts, and your words.

Many people suffer from absorbing the doubts and fears of others, and this needs control too, the recognition first that the energy may not be your own, but has kick started trains of thought that are old, outdated, and past behaviours. It is a continual journey to take control, to decide how you will act, be, think and do.

How do you know if the energy is yours or another's?

It is simple, cleanse the spiritual way, cleanse with nature, ground with spirit and ground with nature and ask is this truly my belief system, is this truly my thinking, is this truly my actions, is this truly how I want to be and stop the emotions that grip you to despair and needless action of uselessness, unworthiness, and misery.

It is not the spiritual way to let others take control of your mind, your essence, and your being. It needs safe guarded, not locked up, but protected the only way a true empath should, with light, with the symbolic light of the creator and with higher energy, so as you carry out your duties and live your life, so you know you are doing this in the footsteps that were pre-determined for you and not for others.

Each chakra requires cleansing each day, new vibrations to enter the aura, an emptying of the aura of unwanted thoughts that are resonating and sitting like muck at the bottom of a dustbin, unwanted thoughts and actions of others that have stuck within you. Clear out your aura of dark energy. Like attracts like and if you do not, more will appear in your life and gather to build a place in the spiritual mind and the physical actions become a torrent of misuse and abuse to oneself and others. It is time to stop being misled by others and journey your own path that is best for your spirit, your physical and your life. This message is for all who entertain the spiritual way as there are many opening up to the way of Spirit and not controlling their energies, being responsible for who they are, light beings.

When you have opened your life and being to a new way of life and being with Spirit, it is highly important to take care of your spiritual being, the aura, the chakras, the spiritual mind, your spirit and keep it clean, grounded in your body and beautiful; think of it as two bodies in one.

Both need to be cleaned, loved, fed, and nourished in equal amounts.

Take the time to do this, and a better course will lay out before you, and those that surround you from the Spirit world can enter and come closer to assist you on your journey, so the words, do not doubt, do not fear, are only words that do not resonate as you trust, you have faith, you know, and you are the light; you are love, and you are the being of the creator and act in His creation on Earth.

Final Thoughts

Thinking is sometimes uncalled for and knowing when not to think is an art form. It is part of letting go, part of connecting with your higher self, to not think. But thoughts can interrupt like the telephone ringing or someone interrupting or your brain working overtime thinking out problems, attitudes, and desires. Let thought go completely to be inspired, to find a higher connection with the divine, and to be inspired. There are many sequences to connecting to Spirit, quietening the mind, and connecting to your own higher self, but there is little knowledge to measure your knowing-ness other than you can feel it with all your being and heart, when you know it or something is right, it speaks to the heart.

Training your whole mind to let go and release thought can seem impossible. But it is not, when you sleep you do not think, you dream yourself into another space and time. When you relax, you let go, to feel the release of the tension in this time and the grip is relaxed. So, now you have to find your heart's desire and to do this, the first step is to stop looking, and connect with your whole heart deep within, so that it emerges out of you in a fully known realisation. This step of relaxing your own being through your gifts and talents is the first step to getting into alignment with you, to be in alignment with the Earth and Spirit, so you can practice the many teachings and guidance within this book.

Do not despair. Feeling despair is the action that will throw out all of your being, misalign thought with feeling, and make you feel helpless in any given situation. Bring in the feeling of security, joy, stability, and hopefulness through the action of being in nature, wonderment, and awe, this will help you raise the vibrations to connect to the elementals, to bring about inspiration. Mother Nature is a great healer along with Spirit.

Being quiet, still and calm is the secret to knowing you and more. Being open, kind, and respectful of all that is in existence is the key to seeing more than what is; to see the truth of your existence, be mindful of all you think.

The expression of like, to like something, to like doing, to like being with, to like feeling will grow your heart to love and respect. Put a value on your likes and loves; value and treasure you.

It is thought that rules and fuels the heart. To find the magic of you, connect your thinking to your heart, make it heart-felt, think and feel from the heart.

Your heart is your love, your happiness, your joy, your smiles, and your gratitude of you. Control and discipline knock out fear and worry. Love and joy are built on trust and faith. Happiness is being in wonder of what is, and peace is the foundation stone to building a life that accepts everything that is.

About RoseAnne

RoseAnne Rosslin is a naturally gifted clairvoyant, medium, psychic, and healer with nearly 30 years of experience who lives in the UK.

RoseAnne became aware of her spirituality in early adulthood when she switched careers to the arts. She embraced and developed her mediumship through training with a spiritual teacher and mentor, which enhanced and propelled her abilities, then led her to help others develop their spiritual gifts.

Whilst RoseAnne is not a medium in the conventional sense that you may know, such as connecting and communicating with Spirit on behalf of someone requiring a reading, instead, it is the other way round. RoseAnne is a medium for the Spirit world, receiving and delivering their messages to people through the written word. However, she gives occasional readings for those who need to hear messages from their loved ones now in Spirit.

To support her life as a medium, RoseAnne lives close to nature and now leads a quiet life surrounded by mountains and the sea. She spends a lot of time writing for Spirit and now, at their request, has released the words into the world.

Books By RoseAnne

The Light of Jesus: A simple guide of truth, spiritual philosophy and wisdom as given by Jesus and the Christ realm.

The Caretaker's Request: Planetary Predictions from a Caring Entity

Further Information

RoseAnne continues to write for the Spirit world. To be notified of her new works and writings, follow RoseAnne on Instagram @roseannerosslin.

If you enjoyed this book, please take a few moments to share your thoughts and insights and write a review on Amazon. Thank you!

Printed in Great Britain
by Amazon

40464977R00056